The Avoidance

Story of Grief, Absence, Fear, and Hope

Misaal

BookLeaf Publishing

India | USA | UK

Made with ❤ on the BookLeaf Publishing Platform
www.bookleafpub.in
www.bookleafpub.com

Dedication

To my first love, Ovais Ahmed Khan a.k.a. Aatish (dad).
I hope you are proud of me.
Love you.

Preface

It's been five years since I lost my father and five years since I stopped writing.

This book is me coming back to both.

I didn't know how to process what I felt. So I didn't. I avoided it. Or maybe I tried to forget in pieces.

This book is not just poetry. It's a sequential autobiography of my emotions, steeped in the long, quiet soup of grief. Each poem is a timestamp, a weather report from within. They trace the shape of loss— sometimes sharp, sometimes vague, always there.

My father was everything. The most beautiful man I've ever known—and I don't say that with the soft bias of a daughter. He was, quite literally, a model. Striking, composed, charismatic. But it was the architecture of his mind that genuinely held me. He had this quiet brilliance, a way of knowing the world so thoroughly it often felt like he'd been here before. He always had an answer, whether I was five and asked why the sky was blue or twenty and unravelling over something I couldn't name. It was not always the one I wanted, but it was always the one I needed.

He fixed things. Objects, emotions, situations— people(especially people). He had that rare ability to absorb chaos and return calm. It was a kind of magic, really. A masculinity built not on power, but on presence. He was strong, visibly so, but it was his steadiness that made me feel safest. He never asked me to be small. He never taught me to seek approval. Instead, he quietly built a foundation in me—self-worth poured from his hands like concrete. And when I doubted myself, which I often did, he reminded me that I was his painting. A masterpiece in progress, but whole even in the unfinished parts.

He listened. Endlessly. I talked in spirals, in tangents, in circles—and he never once looked away. He drank my strange detox teas without question. Helped me design outfits as if he had nothing more pressing to do. He was curious about my world, never mocking, never dismissive. With him, I was never too much. Never too loud, too emotional, too sensitive. I was just... me. And he made that feel like enough.

Even now, with him gone, I don't feel like the story has closed. It's shifted, yes. Quieted. But not ended. He lingers in the background of my thoughts, in the half-sentences I still find myself saying out loud. I still speak to him, without needing a reply. And I truly believe that one day, in some version of the universe more forgiving than this one, we'll find each other again. We'll walk side by side—me talking, like I always did, and him listening, like he always did. Nothing needing to be fixed. Just the two of us, exactly as we were.

If you're reading this and you're grieving too, I want you to know this:

There are uncountable ways to process grief, and none of them are wrong.

Death is inevitable.

And so is moving on.

To everyone who has lost someone and now lives in a cluttered room of emotions—boxes stacked to the ceiling, too heavy to lift, too sacred to throw away. You know that feeling: the dormant black hole in your chest, the one you tiptoe around because you're afraid that if you feel too much, it will consume you.

This is my brave attempt to not just feel it—but to poke it, provoke it, fight with it. To demand something back from the dark. Maybe peace. Maybe understanding. Maybe just a voice again.

Whatever comes, this book is me standing in the doorway of that room, not running anymore.

Acknowledgements

To my mother — the fiercest woman I know — who didn't let the thunderstorm carry me away. Instead, she gave me wings of my own. Your strength held us all together when everything felt like it was falling apart. Thank you for teaching me how to fly through grief.

To my brother, who reminds me so much of Dad — in the way he looks, in the way he moves, in the quiet steadiness of his presence. I hope that one day, you'll remember him the way I do: not just in fragments, but in full color. I hope you'll let yourself feel it all, even the sadness.

To GC — my unwavering support. Thank you for walking beside me through every shadow, never once turning away. You made this unbearable thing bearable. Processing this trauma with you made healing possible.

This book holds pieces of all of you.

1. Haste

*Grief: A moment-by-moment memory of watching death
arrive too fast, too real, and too unfair.*

When I saw you sleep
eyes still open,
I remembered you once said — only horses do that.

A flicker of fear
that maybe you weren't just sleeping
Guilt followed fast, like you knew I'd thought that.

You woke up.
I said "hi."
I didn't know that'd be the last chime.

I stepped outside,
thinking everything was fine.
I didn't know what waited inside

I tried to stay calm,

alert, composed — a silent mime,
though what I saw
felt like a scream through my spine.

I asked you, gently: *Are you fine?*
But you didn't answer. Not this time.

You looked at me
unmoving, unreadable.
And I knew: this day would never leave me.

Never knew it could feel so heavy,
pumping life into someone barely breathing.
But your silence began to grieve me.

I wasn't sure if there was a soul left to see.
Still, I kept trying — like you might come back to me.
Alas! I saw a dilation in your eyes

I'm missing pieces — whole hours vaporized.
Maybe mercy lives where memory dies.
I can't recall the voices, just the thought that you
probably died.

I was angry. Not just sad — *furious.*
Thousands die every single day.
And still, no one had a damn plan.

My mind had already let go.
I needed someone to make it official — to let me stop.
But I hated myself for wanting that kind of permission.

I just wanted to rush the storm.
Skip the waiting, the breaking, the slow unravel.
Grief felt too big to hold in real time.

Rush the grief.
The sharp, endless stabs of missing.
the heart-wrenching, bone-deep lonesome.

Like skipping to the credits.
I didn't ask to keep watching.
After all, aren't movies supposed to end happy?

2. Keepsake

*Grief: A search for something — anything — that could
preserve his presence without feeling like goodbye.*

As unreliable memory is
even for intellects like me
I needed something

Something I could trust
To pull you back into the room with me.
A tether. A token.
An index key

A lock of hair crossed my mind.
Crossed it out, more insane than divine.
Even photos — too final,
Too dead, too quiet.

I needed something softer,
Something truer
A keepsake that wouldn't lie,

That could hold the shape of you
Without turning you into a relic.

Something that wouldn't feel like stealing.
Something that could bring me close
Without making the distance louder
Even if the grief reaches its ceiling.

They said I could kiss you goodbye,
Allowed me one last touch
As if I needed permission
Or maybe I did? Everything was alien

I slipped beneath the blanket's fold,
pressed my cheek against your quiet cold.
Then I laid my palm across your chest
and felt only the echo of absence
a silence so vast it roared.

I catalogued every curve
the arch of your brow,
the curl of hair at your temple,
like cramming for an impossible exam.

I sealed one last kiss to your forehead,
Cold as marble, hard as fate.
Next his hairline, my trembling fingertips traced.

Dead but handsome, my 50 yr old
You'd be proud I still remember the kiss
Afterall I have your brain, that brain as gold
This poem is my candour

3. The Play

*Grief: Grieving amidst the absurdity of social rituals,
false roles, and the strange theater of mourning.*

It's all done.
Done and dusted.
I don't know who I am anymore.
I am just a character, but busted.

Playing in a play I didn't write,
Saying dialogues I didn't revise,
Doing my duties, doing the needful,
Forgetting all about them, and moving on to the sequel.

Didn't I just hit a train?
Am I not still on the tracks?
My breath comes in jolts,
my chest tightly packed.

Memory — that unfaithful mistress.
Memory of my dead father's skin tone.

Doesn't wash away
Doesn't leave me alone

I didn't want to see that transformation.
Forgot what I ate, or if I ate
Except for that morbid information.

Suddenly, the scene has changed.
Characters are more mean.
The dialogues — even strange.

Everyone has an agenda.
Everyone claims to know him more than I do.
Why is everybody competing?
Why is the world so cruel?

Why does my mom keep crying,
In front of people she doesn't know?
Why can't I cry
Even just for show?

Didn't think he held so much together,
Like a tight glue, strengthening wet paper.
It is now degenerating.
His body steadily disintegrating.
The play doesn't make sense anymore.
It's a laughable — all the critics know.

4. I Was Too Young

Grief: The guilt of not letting him in when you had the chance, and the longing to turn back time.

You always said, "Come talk to me,
Not just in pain — just casually."
You longed to be the one I'd call,
The friend who knew the *all* in all.

And though I came when life went wrong,
With heartbreaks harsh and fears too strong,
I never shared the crushes, laughs—
The silly things, the teenage halves.

You asked me soft, with hopeful tone,
"If there's a secret, you're not alone."
But I, too young, kept walls in place,
Not seeing tears behind your face.

I didn't know you needed me,
That I was your safe and only company.

I thought you'd always be around,
So I withheld, and stood my ground.

You were a friend without disguise,
A man with warmth behind his eyes.
And I—a child, proud and naive—
Could never know how much you'd grieve.

Now years have passed, and time is cruel,
And I replay each self-made rule.
The ones that said, "Don't overshare,"
That kept your open heart out there.

Now I recall that gentle frame,
The way you softened, said my name.
And it haunts me most, that pleading tone—
To be your friend, *your only one*.

I wish I told you all I kept,
The dreams I dreamt, the tears I wept.
The boys I liked, the fights I lost,
The silly crushes, heartbreaks tossed.

But now there's silence, no more chance,
No dad to call about romance.
And so I speak these lines too late,
To one who bore my youth's closed gate.

If I could go back, just rewind,
I'd let you into every mind.
But all I have is this regret—
A father's wish, **unmet... unmet.**

5. Regrets

Grief: Every small thing you wish you had done
differently, replayed in loops that never close.

Regrets, regrets — they flood my head,
Each one a stone I should've said.
I blamed myself for what befell,
For not just calling, not as well.

One day I missed your ringing name,
Too lost in chats, too lost in shame.
You needed time, I needed space—
And now I'd trade the world for grace.

You tried to be my truest friend,
But I was distant to the end.
You asked if you could just be near—
I smiled, but didn't let you hear.

I never asked, "*Are you okay?*"
In ways that made you truly stay.

I never made you slow things down,
Or drove you once across the town.

You were so strong, you knew your meds—
A mind that always ran ahead.
You ate the greens, you took long walks,
You cheered me on in all my talks.

You sent me photos from the gym,
Your life, your pride — so full, so trim.
I never thought that I should check,
That strength can break, and hearts deflect.

I didn't book more tests, or seek
What Google said in medical speak.
I didn't fight the what-ifs then—
And now I'd claw to go again.

What kind of child forgets to care,
Just 'cause their parent's always *there*?
I thought you'd never need my shield—
But even giants need to yield.

And now each breath you didn't take
Becomes a wound that doesn't break.
Each minute lost becomes a bell—
That rings with things I didn't tell.

Regrets, regrets — I have a sea.
But none of them set your soul free.
They only sit and softly say,
"You loved him much — just not that way."

6. Still Set for Four

Absence: How absence echoes through daily rituals and makes the ordinary feel unbearable.

Set the table, still for four,
Your jacket waits behind the door.
Everything's here, but not your face—
An empty chair, a missing place.

I call your number, hear no tone,
A habit I can't leave alone.
The silence answers like a scream,
I blink and ask, *"Is this a dream?"*

I won't go out and laugh with you,
No calls when I don't know what to do.
No voice to calm my rising fear,
No *"I've got you"* when storms are near.

I still say, *"Let me check with Dad,"*
Then catch myself—it hits so bad.

You were my shield, my steady hand,
Now I alone must try to stand.

The things you knew, you never said,
They left with you, they're all dead.
And things you shared may fade with time,
Like lyrics lost inside a rhyme.

I want time slow to keep you close,
To memorize what mattered most.
But I want it fast so pain can flee—
This echoing ache inside of me.

Absence doesn't sit in peace,
It roars and never seems to cease.
It hums beneath the light and sound,
And shouts when no one is around.

It rings when I am most alone,
When thought and memory start to drone.
It's not the quiet, soft and bare—
It's every part of you not there.

7. The Blame

Absence: A resistance to those who try to explain or justify death with logic, guilt, or hindsight.

The first time that his heart gave way,
Mine cracked too—but he chose to stay.
And though we feared, we held on tight,
Believed he'd rise, return to light.

The second time, he slipped too far,
No coming back, no beating star.
And that's when voices rose and stung—
With blame sharp-tipped on every tongue.

They said, "*He should've made a will,*"
"*Left lessons, plans, a tax-time skill.*"
"*He should have bought more guarantees.*"
As if love's weight were measured fees.

They spoke as if he planned his fall,
Like death responds to calendar call.

As if he'd stood there, cold and proud,
Refusing help, ignoring crowd.

But no one loves to plan their end,
To list their fears, then sign and send.
He lived, he laughed, he held us close—
He wasn't thinking like a ghost.

They cast their guilt on silent skin,
Then praised themselves for looking in.
But grief is not a blame parade,
And pain's not less when it's well-laid.

They didn't ache when he went cold,
Their tears dried fast, their hands let go.
Yet they spoke loud, like they knew best,
While we just wished his heart could rest.

He didn't fail for not preparing—
He lived with joy, with love, with caring.
And blaming him just fed their pride,
While we stood wrecked from what had died.

So no, I won't rewrite his name,
To suit their comfort, cloak their shame.
He gave us all he ever knew—
And that, to me, is always true.

8. The Reminder

Absence: The universe won't let you forget — even when
you try to move on too soon.

One day, when chaos seemed to sleep,
When skies were soft, and winds ran deep,
I dared to breathe, to face the sun—
Pretend the mourning days were done.

I washed your cup and swept the floor,
Did not glance at your coat by the door.
I smiled at strangers, passed a test—
Convinced myself I'd done my best.

I selfishly, so soft, so slow,
Tried not to feel the undertow.
I whispered, *"Maybe time will mend,"*
Believing grief knew how to end.

But that same night, the heavens cracked,
The trees bent low, the storm came back.

The walls cried out, the lights went dead—
The wind spoke everything I'd fled.

The tower broke, the fields ran red,
And Villy—our horse—was found there, dead.
It felt like God had staged the end,
As if the earth could not pretend.

Maybe I moved too fast, too light,
So sorrow struck again by night.
A cruel reminder, sharp and sly
"You don't get to forget," said the sky.

9. The Return

Absence: What it means to slowly come back to grief,
and allow love to guide your healing.

The storm had warned me — loud and clear,
That moving on was far, not near.
But strength was slipping, breath grew tight,
So I chose numbness over fight.

His photos hid where light won't creep,
A box of ghosts I couldn't keep.
One day, I hoped, I'd dare to see—
But not while pain lived close to me.

I changed my number, fled the past,
Yet kept the phone — his words still last.
Five years have passed, I've read them not,
Each unread line, a landmine thought.

I wished, like in that film I find,
Eternal Sunshine of the Spotless Mind,

That love could leave without its trace—
That grief would vanish, leave no space.

Why do they cast, in every frame,
A father who protects through flame?
And just like that, the ending bleeds—
He dies again to serve our needs.

They all die young — the screen won't lie,
With failing hearts and last goodbyes.
A smell, a song, a food we shared—
The world becomes a mine unpaired.

I ran from triggers far and wide,
But they would wait where tears still hide.
How long till I can stand and say:
"*I'll feel the loss and not decay*"?

And then he came — not Dad, but close,
A sculptor of my shattered prose.
He held the heat, and with his grace,
He helped me see my father's face.

He taught me this: "*You are the light,
Your father's voice, his will, his fight.*"
Through love I found the strength to mend,
To let the story re-ascend.

The one I want my dad to see,
Is now the one who carries *me.*
And though their paths will never meet,
I feel his blessing at my feet.

So if he's watching — near, not gone,
I hope he knows I carry on.
That every piece he left in me
Was shaped by love, and set free.

10. Parallel Lines

Absence: Learning how to live without him, yet feeling his legacy in everything you do.

I can't depend on you anymore,
Though you once made my roots explore.
You taught me strength, to stand alone—
Yet you were always just a phone.

In sickness, trouble, boredom, doubt,
You knew what all the fuss's about.
You healed my heart, and fixed the wall,
Even gadgets — you solved it all.

They say, "*You've got this, you're so wise.*"
I nod, but can't meet my own eyes.
For what I miss is not the deed,
But calling you when thoughts would bleed.

You taught me which pills soothe which ache,
But your warm hand no drug can fake.

You made the cures feel soft, not stern,
A love no textbook could ever learn.

My laptop's dead, the screen's all black,
I check the wires, retrace the track.
An engineer, I hold my ground—
But wish it was your voice I found.

Why must I always now be strong?
Why fix the world, where do I belong?
Then I recall, you live through me,
And strength is now your legacy.

I patch up wounds in those I know,
Like you did when life dealt its blow.
If you were here, you'd rest assured—
Your work in me has long endured.

Funny how you grew broccoli proud,
We scoffed and laughed a bit too loud.
Now that it's me who shops and cooks,
It's the first thing that fills my nook.

Why didn't I help dig that dirt?
Why didn't I heed the food, the shirt?
You said, "*Eat this, it makes you strong,*"
Yet you're not here — so was it wrong?

You can't see I like those things now.
It just took time — I see it how.
But time, that thief, it ran too fast,
And left me yearning for the past.

I hate this cycle, truth be told—
To unlearn warmth, relearn the cold.
To find you right in every part,
Now that you've taken half my heart.

In life you were my axis line,
In loss, you still define my spine.
But in this graph of stars and signs,
We're the same but parted — like two parallel lines.

11. The Fear of Forgetting

Fear: The terror of memory fading — his voice, his touch,
his essence slipping through time.

There was a panic deep in me,
A dread that I might fail to see
The lines that shaped your smiling face—
That time would steal, not just erase.

I'd numbed myself to loss, it's true,
But then I feared forgetting *you*.
Your touch, your laugh, your steady hand—
The memories I could barely stand.

I searched through photos, grain and blur,
But pictures can't contain a *her*,
A *him*, a soul, a breath, a glance—
They freeze the frame but miss the dance.

Your voice—I tried to find a trace,
Some echo locked in time and place.

But every clip, each tape and scene,
Had *you* behind, not in between.

You held the camera at each feast,
So we were framed, but you had ceased
To be the subject, face and smile—
You filmed us all, and stayed awhile.

No videos where you just talked,
No footage where you laughed or walked.
Only call logs, short and spare—
"Where are you?" "Just downstairs."

Those fractured signals, barely real,
Now stitch together what I feel.
I piece your essence, bit by bit,
In pixel, pulse, and voice unlit.

I dreamt that maybe I could train
An AI voice to feel you again—
To feed it chats and facial cues,
And make the past a thing I use.

But still I sometimes can't recall
The way you'd hum, or tease, or stall.
The way you danced, or made that dish—
So I began to write and wish.

I tried to journal, inked with care,
But tears soaked through the lines laid bare.
My grief would flood the page each time—
So now I speak instead of rhyme.

An audio log, where voice won't break—
Except it does, for memory's sake.
Yet still I talk, I talk some more—
About your quirks, your steps, your lore.

If friends grow bored, I understand—
But I must name what time unmanned.
For when I speak, you live again—
In stories told through joy and pain.

Each taste, each joke, each sudden cue—
Rebuilds my sense of all of you.
Not all at once, not crystal clear—
But enough to feel you almost near.

And yet, this terror holds me tight:
That one day I'll forget you right.
Not all at once—but piece by piece—
And that's the grief that doesn't cease.

12. The Cry I Inhabit

Fear: A grief so buried it becomes a part of you —
waiting, always, to erupt.

I am inhabited by a cry—
It doesn't scream, it doesn't sigh.
It curls beneath the day I wear,
And waits for silence, waits for air.

I've pushed it down for far too long,
Pretended nothing's ever wrong.
But pain, when caged, begins to swell—
A trapped voice building in its shell.

I didn't want to feel bereft,
So I denied what I had left.
I told myself, "*He's just not near,*
He's far, not gone. He's somewhere here."

I said, "*He's home, and I'm at school,*"
As if this lie could keep me whole.

As if a myth could wrap the ache,
Or fiction fix the heart that breaks.

I didn't want to be the girl
With loss carved deep into her world.
I didn't want my pain to show,
So I erased what made it grow.

There's hibernation in my chest,
A winter sleep of all the rest—
The memories I chose to skip,
The truth I held with loosened grip.

Avoidance is its own disguise,
A shield built from imagined lies.
It lets you smile, go through the day,
While all your insides drift away.

For years I walked without a name
For what I'd lost, or who to blame.
I just pretended I forgot—
That grief was something I was not.

But grief remembers. Grief returns.
It waits in songs, in smells, in turns.
And when it wakes, it shakes the floor—
A cry that can't be caged no more.

13. The Curse of Avoidance

*Fear: How refusing to feel creates its own kind of
suffering — hollow and consuming.*

Because I'd taught my heart to hide,
The grief returned from deep inside.
Not with a knock, but like a wave—
So quiet, yet it wouldn't behave.

The nights grew long, the silence screamed,
I feared the hours I once deemed
So peaceful, still — now filled with dread,
Where echoes crawled inside my head.

My pillow changed, but not its fate—
Still soaked with tears I couldn't state.
The sobs came softly, sharp and slow,
And only darkness saw them grow.

I feared the mornings, feared the nights,
Feared every moment without lights.

The hush would haunt me like a ghost—
The kind of pain that stings the most.

The shower was my hiding place,
A space to cry and not lose face.
I let the water blur my cries,
But no flood cleans the soul's goodbyes.

It rinsed my cheeks, but not my grief,
Each rinse became a new motif—
Of how I tried to wash the ache,
And only made more room to break.

Avoidance kept the pain at bay,
But never taught it how to stay.
So when it came, it carved me wide—
A hollowness I couldn't hide.

14. The Etiquette of Grief

*Fear: Is grief too loud, too selfish, too long-lasting — or is
it just honest?*

Is it selfish that I'm still not whole,
That years have passed but not my soul?
That trauma lingers, deep and wide,
While others laugh with ease outside?

Is it unfair, this heavy heart,
That drags the ones who play their part?
Should they be free from shadows mine,
Just 'cause their skies still get to shine?

I wonder if I dim the room,
Just by existing in my gloom.
If my cracked voice, my sleepless eyes
Make joy in others slowly die.

But would I lie to save their peace,
And trade my truth for brief release?

Would hiding all that aches inside
Make me more kind, or just denied?

They say, "*You're strong*," and I just nod—
Yet breaking shouldn't feel so flawed.
There is no rule, no grief-manual's chart
To teach a fractured how to restart.

Why must this pain define my tone?
Why does it deepen when alone?
And why does every scent or song
Still prove my timeline's moving wrong?

Is sadness self-absorbed, I ask,
Or just the heart without a mask?
If grief's a sea I'm sailing through,
Must I pretend I'm dry for you?

15. Questions and Questions

*Fear: When belief fails to offer certainty, we hold onto
the kind of love we know he would choose.*

What is life... what is death?
I never gave it much thought, never held my breath.
The afterlife? A blank, uncharted map,
And I, the researcher, won't fall for a trap.

I believe in theories, yes, in reason, in proof—
Not in comfort dressed as some heavenly truth.
And yet some nights, I break that mold,
And wonder: can he see me grow old?

Can he see the good? The shameful, too?
Does he watch me win? Does he flinch when I lose?
I tell myself he's still nearby,
Not roaming distant stars in some gilded sky.

Because one thing I know, as sure as air:
He loved us too much to go elsewhere.

Even freed from his body, from pain and time,
He wouldn't chase peace and leave us behind.

No heaven could tempt him far away—
He'd stay right here, come night or day.
No gates of gold, no skyward dome
Could feel as sacred as his home.

He wouldn't start fresh, wouldn't roam,
He'd watch over his family, close to home.
And so—if I don't feel him near—
It leaves me two conclusions, crystal clear:

(a) Perhaps his memory's been erased,
His soul reborn in another place.
Not the worst fate, I admit—
But what if we forget each other bit by bit?

And when we meet, post death's disguise,
Will it even count without the ties?
If love is lost to life's reset,
Are we really us when we forget?

(b) Or worse — that there's no after at all,
Just dirt, decay, a final fall.
No "hello again," no second chance,
Just bones returning to the earth's expanse.

That thought... it cuts through breath and bone,
To think he's gone, and we're alone.
To think we'll never walk again,
Buy that ice cream, laugh in rain.

So for my own heart to survive this storm,
I give belief a softer form.
I say: he's here, he's by my side—
Walking with me through every tide.

And when I die, we'll meet again,
Two old souls with time to spend.
And he'll buy me ice cream both ways, you know,
Like he used to — to and fro.

Until then, I stay and breathe,
With thoughts that circle, never leave.
No answers come. Just endless spins...
I'm left with questions and questions... and questions
again.

16. Runaway Memory

*Fear: Not everyone wants to revisit the past — some need
distance to preserve what they remember.*

Many seek comfort in old things—
The homes, the shirts, the wedding rings.
But I recoil from place and sound,
Where ghosts of him still hang around.

I don't want to live in that house,
Don't want to roam that same old town.
The walls still whisper what I saw,
The silence there still holds its claw.

I don't want someone saying his name
With cheerful tone or shallow claim.
I don't want memories thrown around
Like casual stories in a crowd.

I hate the breaking that must be done
In front of people, one by one.

The sobs that rise without control,
When strangers say, "He had a soul."

I want to go where none have known
The man I lost, the seed he'd sown.
Where I alone can write his lines,
Unspoiled by others' flawed designs.

Let me keep his gentle pride,
His love for horses, fierce yet wide.
His mind — oh God, that brilliant spark,
That lit up systems in the dark.

He built, he grew, he made things bloom,
While others merely filled a room.
He knew computers like they breathed,
And crops obeyed what he conceived.

But I won't chase the fields he loved,
Or live inside the house he shoved
With all his ideas, bolts and wires—
I fear what memory requires.

For what if something breaks that spell?
What if one comment, one small yell
Distorts the way I saw his gaze—
And blurs the sacred in his ways?

So I just run. And keep on running.
Away from echoes, grief, becoming.
I don't want comfort if it risks
Unwriting all his fingerprints.

17. The Cottonwood Theory

*Hope: A personal myth that grief transforms into a quiet
sign — a way to keep him near.*

I thought I'd lost you — truly gone,
No whisper left to lean upon.
The afterlife? I'm torn in two—
I question all, but doubt no view.

As agnostic as I claim to be,
I test each truth like gravity.
Like every theory ever made—
It holds... until it's unafraid.

So maybe you are near, not far—
A silent breeze, a watching star?
But dreams feel silly, shadows play,
And prayers I never quite could say.

Then I thought, if you still exist,
Shouldn't the afterlife have a twist?

Some power left for you to be
A sign that only I would see?

So I picked something soft, not loud—
Not thunder, nor a bursting cloud.
But cottonwoods — they float, they glide,
They're easy missed, but still abide.

They drift like thoughts you used to share,
They dance like you — so light, so rare.
I told myself, *"He lives in these,"*
And found some form of inner peace.

It was just a tale I made to cope,
A child's trick, a fragile hope.
Until one day, the world went still—
And fate had tested deeper will.

My brother called — said, *"Mom has slipped."*
Her health, her strength, both had been stripped.
She didn't call — thought I'm too busy,
Like family's not worth breaking dizzy.

I didn't know if I should run,
If morning flight would beat the sun.
But as my tears fell down, unsure,
A cottonwood came to reassure.

It landed gently on my knee,
Like it had floated just for me.
And in that moment, grief was grace—
Your voice had found another place.

Since then I've known, or liked to think,
You're in that breeze, that airborne wink.
And every time I need a sign,
A cottonwood says, "*You're still mine.*"

18. I Wish You Could See Me

*Hope: All the milestones reached without him, and the
ache of success in his absence.*

You worked your whole life, never slow,
With quiet strength and steady glow.
You failed, you tried, you stood up tall—
And somehow smiled through it all.

Your patience was your truest friend,
A grit that never knew an end.
While I would break at slightest storm,
You weathered life like it was norm.

You saw me lost, unsure, and low,
Unsure of where I'd even go.
You said, *"Life works out in the end,"*
But I was too young to comprehend.

I wish you'd seen what I became,

A heart less fearful, mind aflame.
Now I believe in things unknown,
And trace that strength back to your own.

You longed to see a world so wide,
To chase your dreams, not step aside.
But duty called and you complied—
Your wings stayed folded deep inside.

A year post you, life tore apart,
But then it healed — a braver heart.
I found my place, a PhD,
In halls you'd brag about for me.

At times the joy cuts like a knife—
You couldn't see this part of life.
Couldn't boast to friends with pride,
"Do you know where my child applied?"

I went abroad, just like you dreamed,
Achieved the things you once had schemed.
Yet every win, each accolade,
Felt softer in your absent shade.

Sometimes I think you pull the strings,
That you're the wind beneath my wings.
And still I ask — is it too much,

To want your hand, your unseen touch?

But if there's rest beyond the skies,
A place where quiet mercy lies,
Then let me set your spirit free—
Don't haunt the earth to comfort me.

I wish you'd see me wedding-bound,
With children running all around.
But if your peace is far from here,
Then let that be — and I'll stay near.

I'll never see your silvered hair,
Or walk you slow from here to there.
But maybe that's your gift to me—
To only hold your strength in memory.

You left too soon, yet somehow stayed,
In every choice I've ever made.
And since I never saw you gray,
You'll be my young superhero — always that way.

19. Love and everything in Between

Hope: A father's love, shown in the quietest, strongest ways — a blueprint for how to be loved.

My father never said what love was.
He showed me—
in school uniforms warmed on cold mornings,
in boiled eggs cooked soft
so I'd grow tall,
in quiet tasks done with devotion,
never announced,
just done.

He taught me love was action—
a steady rhythm,
not grand but constant.
A presence that moved
without being asked.
That love was not in how loud you speak
but in how silently you show up.

He wasn't perfect—
not always the partner my mother needed—
but as a father,
I saw love in its purest form.

I saw it
when she was unwell.
He cleaned, changed diapers,
held my baby brother,
and cooked three different meals—
for her ill stomach,
for my frail brother,
and for me.
Each plate made with care,
no shortcuts, no fuss.
He fed us like it was sacred.

That was his love:
calm, capable, without complaint.
A hand on the world
without asking it to applaud.

When I had my accident,
I didn't cry—
not until I saw him.

He arrived faster than physics allows,
a rose in hand,
his eyes scanning for the pain
before I could even name it.

That's when I let go.
That's when I sobbed.
Because his presence meant
I could finally break.

He was always the place
where I didn't have to be brave,
where being small was safe.

He taught me what I deserve.
He set the bar.
And now I carry that standard
like a watermark on my spirit.

So if someone asks
what kind of love I'm looking for,
I'll say:

**Give me the kind of love
that brings a rose
to an accident.
Give me the kind of love**

that boils milk
while holding a baby.
Give me the kind of love
that cooks three meals
to keep a family steady.
Give me the kind of love
that warms the dress
before wearing.
Because that's how
my father showed me.

20. Something Sweet

*Hope: Letting grief shape you into something deeper,
kinder — like sugar that must burn to sweeten.*

I never understood
how he could be so lively—
so gentle in his laughter,
so generous with time,
so soft with every little part of me.

But maybe
he too had seen death
before he was ready.
Maybe he lost someone he loved
too soon,
and maybe that grief
never really left him.

Maybe it shaped him—
not into steel,
but into something

that bent toward kindness.
Something thoughtful.
Something open.

I look at my own sorrow
and wonder if it could do the same—
if this ache could soften me,
refine me,
make me more alive,
not less.

Some things, after all,
require heat
to taste like heaven.
**A dessert must go through flame
to become its sweetest self.**
Sugar doesn't melt
into anything beautiful
until it's burned just a little.

Maybe that's what grief does—
it melts what's hard,
caramelizes the raw,
and leaves behind
something richer
than it found.

So I'll try.
I'll try to let this pain
make me more like him—
thoughtful,
sensitive,
capable of loving so deeply
it startles people.

And as I carry his memory forward,
I'll keep reminding myself:

Just because someone is dead,
doesn't mean they were always right.
But it doesn't mean they were wrong either.
They were human.
They lived.
They tried.
And so will I.

21. The Avoidance

The final reckoning: that the only way out of grief is
through it — again, and again, and again.

I avoided this grief
for five long years—
tucked it beneath work,
beneath smiles,
beneath a practiced kind of strength
that even I believed sometimes.

But writing this book
was opening the floodgates.
Not just a slow leak—
but a flood,
a hailstorm,
an earthquake
one after the other.

It shook memories loose
I thought I'd preserved.

It cracked parts of me
I thought were healed.
It brought back his voice in echoes,
his face in flashes,
and pieces of me
I hadn't met in years.

Some memories came back wrong.
Some, I'd already forgotten.
And some days,
I lost myself so completely
I wondered
if I would ever come back.

But here's the one thing I know now—
the truth I was running from:

Avoidance is not mercy.
It is a trickster.
A seducer.
A satin-lined cage.

It whispers,
"You're okay now."
And just when you exhale,
it pokes your soul
like a cruel child

playing with an old wound.

Avoidance doesn't save you.
It just delays the collapse.
And every delay makes the fall
so much harder to survive.

If there's a path out,
if there's a way through,
it is this:

Feel it.
All of it.
All at once.
All the time.
More than once.

Feel it until the sharp becomes soft.
Until the ache folds into shape.
Until your tears no longer burn—
but bless.

That is grief.
That is recovery.
That is love
wearing its truest face.